The License Plate Game Book

40 Great Travel Games for Fun on the Go!

Michael Teitelbaum and James Buckley, Jr.

ISBN 0-8167-5632-5

Printed in the United States of America.

10 9 8 7 6 5 4 3 2 1

Produced by Creative Media Applications
Art Direction by Fabia Wargin Design

Table of Contents

Look in the back of the book for your license plate stickers.

Rules of the Road

NO PASSING ZONE

Have you ever taken a long car trip? Well, if you have, you know that whoever said, "Getting there is half the fun," probably never rode in the backseat of the car with a bunch of brothers and sisters! Car trips can sometimes be long and boring.

But they don't have to be.

With some imagination (and this book, of course), you can turn your next drive into a trip to the funhouse.

To play most of the games in this book, all you need are your eyes and ears. For others, you need paper and something to write with. And for a few, a deck of playing cards comes in handy. The directions for each game tell you everything you need to play.

But don't just do what we tell you to do. Make up your own games—or change the rules to these games to fit your family's idea of fun. You'll probably use a road map to get where you're going—but as you can see on any map, there are lots of different ways to get to the same place. In addition to these games, tell stories; make up fairy tales; ask your parents about what they were like as kids; try to name all the words you know starting with Z (okay, maybe this last one won't kill a lot of time).

This fun-filled book also contains stickers of the license plates of all 50 states and all of the Canadian provinces. In the first activity—*Plates, Plates, and More Plates*—you'll get to place the sticker of each license plate you spot into its space in the book.

So dive right in. Who knows? You may have so much fun in the car that you'll never even ask that famous question: "Are we there yet?..."

Plates, Plates, and More Plates

"Does Washington, D.C., count as a state?"

EQUIPMENT: The 62 license plate stickers found at the back of this book; sharp eyes and clean windows

TO PLAY: Everyone in the car looks out the window searching for license plates. When a plate is spotted, take the sticker for that license plate from the sticker page in this book and place it in the corresponding box. Continue trying to fill gaps in your plate-spotting collection throughout your trip.

OTHER IDEAS: Draw a star by the states and provinces you drive through, and you'll have a permanent record of your travels.

Washington, D.C., isn't a state, but it has its own plate!

U.S. States

Alabama	Alaska	Arizona	Arkansas	California
Colorado	Connecticut	Delaware	Florida	Georgia
Hawaii	Idaho	Illinois	Indiana	Iowa

Kansas	Kentucky	Louisiana	Maine	Maryland
Massachusetts	Michigan	Minnesota	Mississippi	Missouri
Montana	Nebraska	Nevada	New Hampshire	New Jersey
New Mexico	New York	North Carolina	North Dakota	Ohio
Oklahoma	Oregon	Pennsylvania	Rhode Island	South Carolina
South Dakota	Tennessee	Texas	Utah	Vermont
Virginia	Washington	West Virginia	Wisconsin	Wyoming

Canadian Provinces

			Alberta	British Columbia
Manitoba	New Brunswick	Newfoundland & Labrador	Nova Scotia	Ontario
Prince Edward Island	Quebec	Saskatchewan	The Klondike	Northwest Territories

First Flag

"Flag light, flag bright, first flag I see tonight."

EQUIPMENT: None

TO PLAY: Look for flags, any flags—U.S. flags, gas station flags, state flags, flags on buildings, flags on other cars, any flag you see. If you're the first player to see a particular flag, shout, "Flag!" and get one point. If two people shout "Flag!" at the same time, no one gets a point for that flag. The first player to get ten points is the winner; you can play as many rounds as you want.

OTHER IDEAS:

- Instead of playing for points, play for colors. Each player has to find flags that contain at least one of these colors: red, white, blue, green, yellow, orange, purple. Each flag can count for only one color (so the U.S. flag doesn't count for three).
- Look for groups of flags—pairs, threes, or more; whoever can spot the most flags flying together within ten minutes or ten miles wins.

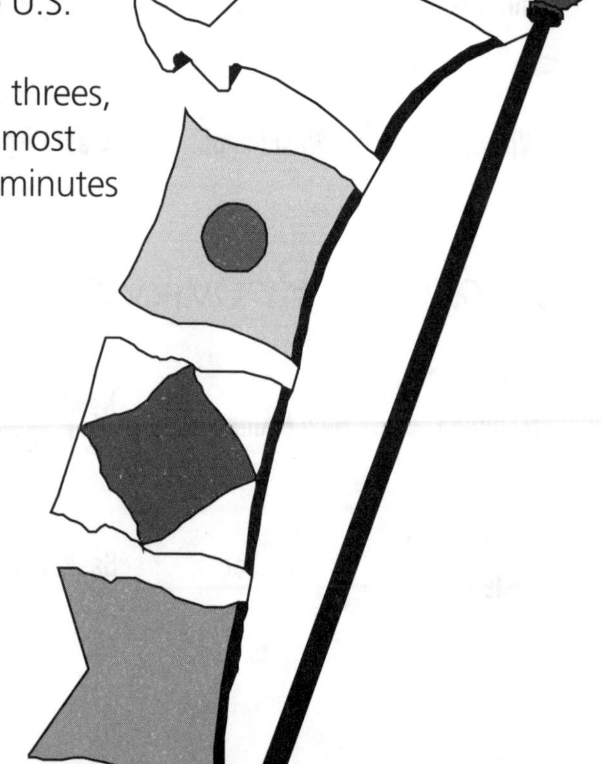

I Pick Infinity

"Gimme a 1, gimme a 2, gimme a 3..."

EQUIPMENT: None

TO BEGIN: Each player picks a side of the car to look from. Also, pick a number above ten that you'll be playing to. Don't pick infinity! Your trip can't be that long, even if it feels that way sometimes!

FUN FACT

President Eisenhower signed a bill in 1956 that started the Interstate Highway System. He was inspired to build the interstate highways because of a trip he took while in the army. In 1911, he and hundreds of soldiers took 62 days to cross the United States by car and truck. Today, you could do it in three... if you really had to.

TO PLAY: The object of the game is to find numbers in order. The numbers can be on signs or license plates or anywhere. You have to find each number in order. That means if you see a 4 before you've seen a 3, it doesn't count. Each player starts at 1 and goes up. The first one to get to the chosen number is the winner.

OTHER IDEAS:

- Play in reverse; start with 15 or 20 and count down to 1.
- Play odds and evens; one person has to find odds (1, 3, 5, 7...), the other person has to find evens (2, 4, 6, 8...).
- Play fives to 100 (5, 10, 15, 20...).

Personal Plates

"Dad, that car's license plate says 'ROCKSTAR.' Can we stop and ask for an autograph?"

EQUIPMENT: Sharp eyes and some quick thinking

TO BEGIN: Do you know what a personalized license plate is? In most states, owners of cars can choose what letters and numbers they want on their license plates, as long as the same letters and numbers aren't already on another car. People can put their names, their dogs' names, funny slogans or sayings, or their jobs on their plates. Those special plates are what you're looking for in this game.

TO PLAY: Just look for plates that spell things. Many people use abbreviations. Some of the most popular abbreviations are:

- 8 for any "ate" sound (GR8 = great)
- 2 for "to" or "too" (2N = tune)
- M = am
- IM = I am
- 4 = for (IM4U)
- Also look for shortened words, such as LV for "love," FL for "full," or MR for "mister." See who can find the funniest personalized plate.

EXAMPLES:

Occupations:

ILVIT8—Magician (I levitate)
IFXCARZ—Mechanic (I fix cars)
IW8—Waiter (I wait)
IMLAW—Policeman (I am law)

Other examples include:

10SE (Tennessee) and IMAQT (I'm a cutie). Sideshow Bob on *The Simpsons* has a license plate that says IH8BART (I hate Bart). Can you think of others?

I Sentence You...

"'I yield gas highway diner.' Is that a sentence?"

EQUIPMENT: Paper; pencil or pen

TO BEGIN: Look for words out your window and write down as many as you can in three minutes. The words can be long or short. Don't forget to look for verbs!

TO PLAY: Make up as many sentences as you can using only the words you see out your window. The words can be on signs, on trucks—on anything you see. The stranger or funnier the sentence, the better. If you want to make it a competition, see who can come up with a five-word sentence first. Then try to make longer sentences.

Bumper-Sticker Bonanza

"There's one: 'My Kid Is a Star Bumper-Sticker Spotter!'"

EQUIPMENT: None, unless you want to draw your own bumper stickers (see Other Ideas)

TO BEGIN: Each player picks one side of the car to look from. Keep your eyes peeled!

TO PLAY: Count as many bumper stickers as you can in ten miles. Players get one point for each bumper sticker they spot. Whoever spots the most is the winner.

OTHER IDEAS:

- Read the bumper stickers aloud as you see them. If you can make your opponent laugh at any of the stickers you see, you get an extra point.
- Draw or write your own bumper stickers. Think silly!
- Count bumper stickers in different categories: political candidates, tourist attractions, sports teams, radio stations, silly slogans, and so on.

Geo-Alphabet

"A is for Alabama. B is for Broadway. C is for Kentucky. Oops! That's a K."

EQUIPMENT: Paper; pencil or pen

TO PLAY: Check out every road sign and highway mileage sign you see. Using only place names that you see out the window, try to find one place starting with every letter of the alphabet. You can skip X and Z if you want; there aren't many place names that begin with these. This is a good game to play over the course of a long trip, so start a page on your pad of paper and go back to it each day of the trip. While you're playing other games, you can still look for any letters you're missing on the Geo-Alphabet list.

FUN FACT

Want to see the World's Largest Catsup Bottle? It's 70 feet tall and can be seen near Collinsville, Illinois. Unfortunately, the World's Largest French Fries are not nearby.

OTHER IDEAS:

- To make it really hard, use only street names or city names to fill your alphabet.
- Narrow the list to places that have more than five or six letters in their names.
- Here's a tricky one: fill your alphabet list with words that *end* in A, B, C, and so on.

Spell-It

"I've got an X, a Q, a Z, and an O.
What in the world can I spell with that?"

EQUIPMENT: Paper; pencil or pen for each player

TO PLAY: Looking at license plates, each player writes down the first letter from the next ten plates he or she sees. Once everyone has ten letters, see who can make up the most words from his or her ten letters in the next five miles. All the words have to be at least three letters long. Whoever comes up with the most words is the winner.

OTHER IDEAS:

- Make up nonsense words out of your letters. Come up with a nonsense word and then try to see who can make up the funniest "daffy-nition."
- To make it harder, play with more letters—say 15 or 20—or make a rule that words have to be at least four letters long.

FUN FACT

If you're on an interstate highway, the higher the number, the farther north or east you are. The lower the number, the farther south or west you are. And if the number is divisible by 5 or 10, it's a good bet it's a long and important highway.

FUN FACT

Why are interstate road signs green and white? In 1957, the government held a test, and more drivers liked those colors. The other choices had been blue and black, each with white letters.

Miles of Math

"I just saw a plate that said 9999.
I think I'm going to win."

EQUIPMENT: Paper; pencil or pen for each player; someone who can add (or a calculator)

TO PLAY: Each player writes down all the numbers from the next five license plates he or she sees. Then each player adds his or her numbers up, one digit at a time. Whoever has the highest total wins. You can play five or ten rounds and see who comes up with the highest grand total.

FUN FACT

All the roads in the United States laid end to end would circle the earth 175 times!

OTHER IDEAS:

- Most license plates have groups of numbers and groups of letters. Instead of adding the numbers one digit at a time, add the groups. If a plate reads "849-MTE," use 849 as your number, not 8 plus 4 plus 9.
- Look for license plates that have a number group that starts with a 1, a 2, a 3, and so on (175, 234, 397…). When everyone has a group of numbers starting with 1 through 9, add them up and see who wins.

What Am I Counting?

"I hope you guys guess this soon...
I keep seeing a lot of cows. Oops! Gave it away!"

EQUIPMENT: None

TO BEGIN: Decide who will go first in this guessing game.

TO PLAY: One player picks something that everyone can see out the window, but he or she doesn't tell the other players what it is he or she is looking at. Every time the player whose turn it is sees another of the thing he or she is looking for, that player counts aloud. For instance, if your secret thing is white trucks, say, "One," when you see the first white truck, then, "Two," when you see the second, and so on. The other players must guess what it is you are counting. As soon as one of the other players guesses what is being counted, that person becomes the counter.

OTHER IDEAS:

- Narrow the game down by picking only things seen out of one side of the car.
- If no one guesses after a while, let the players ask a yes-or-no question to try to get a clue about what is being counted. If they can't guess it after three questions, the counter wins.

HINTS AND EXAMPLES: Try to pick things you'll probably see often as you drive. For example, choose all gas station signs, not just ones that say "Bob's Gas & Feed." There might not be another one of those for hundreds of miles!

Some other sorts of things you can count are barns, specific types or colors of cars, bridges, trucks, fast-food restaurants, flags, or boats.

What's Coming Down the Road?

"The next car we see will be a purple polka-dot V.W. micro-bus!"

EQUIPMENT: None

TO PLAY: This game is played best on a winding, curvy road. As you approach a curve in the road, everyone has to guess the color of the next vehicle coming the other way. Whoever guesses right gets one point. You can play to as many points as you want.

OTHER IDEAS:

- Instead of colors, try types of vehicles (trucks, sedans, sport utility vehicles, minivans, station wagons, motorcycles, and so on).
- You can also try guessing brands of cars, especially if you're all auto experts (Ford, Buick, Volkswagen, Volvo, Subaru, and so on).
- You can play this game on a road with hills or rises up ahead, too. Use the next car that comes over the hill in front of you as the correct answer.

FUN FACT

Under Interstate 75 in Florida, there is a special tunnel just for Florida panthers to walk through. Why does the panther cross the road? He doesn't have to... he uses the tunnel.

Backseat Bingo

"Speed up, Dad. All I need for bingo is a policeman on a motorcycle."

EQUIPMENT: Paper; pencil or pen for each player

TO BEGIN: Each player draws a square grid of 16 boxes (4 rows of 4 boxes each) on a piece of paper. In each box, write the name of something you might see out the window of the car. Some examples are listed below, but use your imagination. Don't make it impossible (no flying saucers, for example, unless you're near Roswell, New Mexico), because you might end up with that grid yourself.

Once each player has filled in a grid, put them all facedown in a pile and shuffle. Each player then chooses one grid at random. It's okay if you get your own grid.

TO PLAY: Players look out the window and try to spot the things written on their grid. They mark each item they find with an X. If you get four X's in a row, either up and down, across, or diagonally, yell, "BINGO!" You're the winner! But don't yell too loudly—you'll startle the driver!

HINTS AND EXAMPLES: Possible words for your grids are: barn, billboard, water tower, gas station, orange cone, office building, parking lot, bus, motorcycle, cow, flower garden, bicycle, truck, RV, police car.

house	red car	cow	pig
bull-dozer	bill-board	exit sign	barn
gas station	no-passing sign	RV	phone booth
road kill	motor-cycle	flowers	hawk

Car Categories

"There's no way you wrote down the names of fourteen planets!"

EQUIPMENT: Paper; pencil or pen for each player; a watch or clock

TO BEGIN: Have everyone think of a bunch of categories, such as birds, fruit, countries, or types of cars (for more category ideas, see Hints and Examples below). Write them on individual slips of paper. Then mix up the papers. (To keep things interesting, write out new categories each time you play.)

TO PLAY: Each player draws a category from the pile of papers. With someone keeping time, players have five minutes to write down as many things as possible that fit into the category they have chosen. After five minutes are up, score one point for each word that fits the category, but take away two points for any words that don't fit. Whoever has the most points wins. Play as many rounds as you want.

OTHER IDEAS:

- Instead of playing by the clock, play by the odometer. Whoever gets the most points in five miles or ten miles wins.
- After a person picks a category, have everyone work together to think of one word for that category beginning with A, another beginning with B, and so forth for each letter of the alphabet.

HINTS AND EXAMPLES: Some categories to get you started are: birds, fruits, countries, types of cars, adjectives, furniture, names of your friends, foods, sports equipment, islands, state capitals, colors, movies starring animals.

Cross-Street Dots Game

"I've got you lined up right where I want you!"

EQUIPMENT: Paper; pencil or pen

TO BEGIN: Draw a grid made of rows and columns of dots. The grid can be as big or small as you want. It can be a square or a rectangle. See below for an example.

TO PLAY: Each player in turn draws one horizontal or vertical line connecting two dots. No diagonal lines. The object for each player is to try to draw the line that completes a square of four dots. When you do that, write your initial in the square. The person with the most squares when the grid is completed is the winner.

HINTS AND EXAMPLES: The key to this dots game is to make your opponent draw the third line in a square. Then you can draw the fourth one. Watch for chances to draw one line that makes two squares; that's a great way to get two points with one line. This is a game of strategy and patience. The more you play, the better you'll be.

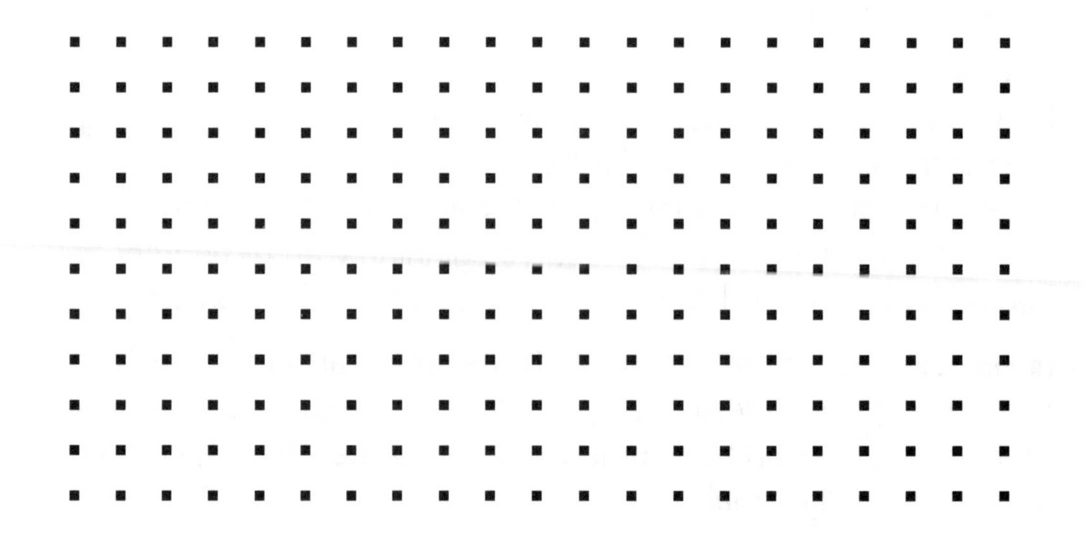

Tic-Tac-Toe Tourney

"I've seen the X-Files, but what about the O-Files?"

EQUIPMENT: A single big pad of paper; pencil or pen for each player

TO BEGIN: The more people you have, the more fun this is. Draw as many tic-tac-toe grids as you want. Decide who will play against whom in the first round.

TO PLAY: This is a best-of-ten-games tournament. The first-round winners move on to the championship finals. Use the regular tic-tac-toe rules: One player is X and one player is O. Alternate filling in the grid until one player has three in a row, up and down, across, or diagonally. Ties don't count in this tournament. Make sure to take turns going first in each game. The first player to win six games wins the round.

FUN FACT

The longest road in the world is the Pan American Highway. It stretches from Alaska to Chile.

OTHER IDEAS:

- If you have only three players, play a round-robin. Each player takes on the other two players in turn. The two players who win the most games play off for the championship.
- Try "random" tic-tac-toe. Make the grid large enough to fill your page. Then close your eyes and wave your pencil over the grid before you pick a square—without looking!
- Keep a running total over the course of a long drive. Make it like a football season, with the top "teams" going to the Tic-Tac-Toe Super Bowl.
- Find a really ugly souvenir and make it the tic-tac-toe trophy. The winner gets to keep the trophy until he or she is defeated.

Highway Hangman

"Hmm. A three-letter word ending in AR.
And you say it's something I've seen out the window?"

EQUIPMENT: A single pad of paper; pencil or pen for each player

TO BEGIN: This game is played like regular hangman. One player chooses a secret word and draws blank lines, one for each letter in the word. In this version, however, the secret word should be only something seen out the car window.

TO PLAY: The other players take turns guessing letters. If a letter is in the word, the player who chose the word writes that letter in the correct blank, and the person who guessed the letter tries to guess the word. If the letter is not in the word, it's written down to show it has been used. Then a body part is added to the hanging post in this order: head, body, two arms, and two legs. You can add hands, feet, eyes, and a mouth if you want to allow more guesses. If a player guesses the secret word before the body is complete, he or she wins. If not…it's hangman!

HINTS AND EXAMPLES: If you're guessing, try vowels first: A, E, I, O, and U. They're used most often. Some of the most popular consonants are S, L, M, T, and R. If you're choosing the secret word, try a word with strange letters, such as X, Q, or Z, to make the guessing tougher.

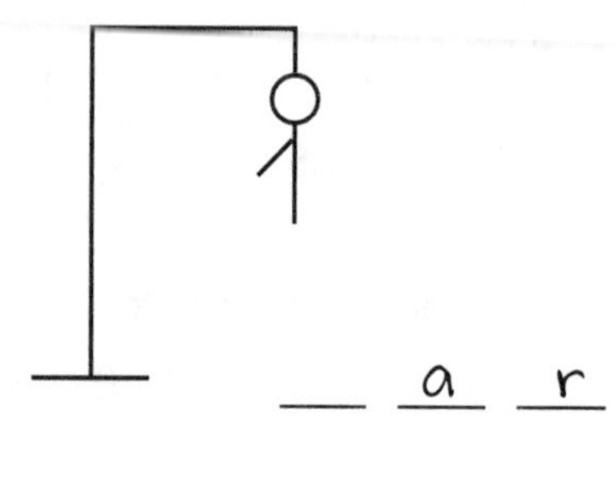

Map Mania

"Name a square state? You'll have to be more specific."

EQUIPMENT: A map of the United States or Canada; paper and pencil or pen for keeping score

TO BEGIN: Choose one player to be the first "mapmaker." Each person will take a turn being the mapmaker.

TO PLAY: The mapmaker asks the other players five questions, all based on the map, such as: "What state has the most S's in its name?" "How many states' names start with the word *New*?" or "Which province is between British Columbia and Saskatchewan?" You get one point each time you are the first to correctly answer the mapmaker's question. Play as many rounds as you like.

HINTS AND EXAMPLES: You can ask questions about states' and provinces' sizes, shapes, locations, capitals, colors (on your particular map), names, or anything else you can see on the map. You can ask about rivers and mountain ranges. You can ask about major highways (if they show up on your map). You can ask anything, as long as the other players can find the answers on the map, which everyone shares. Be creative! You're the mapmaker!

OTHER IDEAS:

- Give each round of questions a theme. For instance, in the first round, perhaps all the questions could be related to the names of the states or provinces, such as "What state has only four letters in its name?" or "Name the only two provinces that begin and end with a vowel." In the second round, perhaps all the questions might relate to the locations of states and provinces, such as "What province is on the border of Michigan?"
- Use a map of the United States *and* Canada to make the game harder.

Name Game

"Ignatz is a real name!"

EQUIPMENT: Paper; pencil or pen

TO BEGIN: Decide upon the order of play.

TO PLAY: Each player in turn says a first name. The first player must say a name starting with A; the second player must say a name starting with B; the third player must say a name starting with C; and so on, all the way through the alphabet. (You can skip X and Q if you want, and maybe even skip Y and Z; there aren't many names that begin with these letters.) When you get to the end of the alphabet, start again with A. Write down each name as someone says it. The round ends when one player can't come up with a name for his or her letter; use the list you make to keep people from repeating names. Play as many rounds as you like.

HINTS AND EXAMPLES:

Here is a sample for the first six letters in a round of names.

A Albert B Betty C Carl
D Donna E Eddie F Francis

OTHER IDEAS:

- Alternate boys' names and girls' names (the way hurricanes are named). A should be a boy's name, B should be a girl's name, C should be a boy's name, and so on. Names that work for both boys and girls, such as Alex or Pat, count for either.
- Play backward, starting with Z and ending with A.

First and Last

"Mom? Can you think of any more countries that start with Z?"

EQUIPMENT: Paper; pencil or pen

TO BEGIN: Decide upon the order of play. Then choose a category, such as countries, cities, foods, or rock groups (for more category ideas, see Hints and Examples below).

TO PLAY: Players take turns naming an example of the chosen category. The trick is that each word must begin with the last letter of the previous word. For instance, if your category is *countries*, here is what the first four players might say: France, England, Denmark, Kuwait. The last letter in "France" is E, so the next word starts with E: "England." Get it? The round is over when a player cannot keep the pattern going. Write down the words that are used to avoid repeats.

OTHER IDEAS:

- In alternating rounds, players do "First and Last," then "All First"; for example, Round 1: France, England, Denmark, Kuwait; Round 2: Bolivia, Brazil, Bangladesh, Belgium; Round 3: back to "First and Last."

HINTS AND EXAMPLES: Some ideas for categories are: countries, cities, foods, rock groups, song titles, famous actors, sports stars, colors, animals, birds, and insects.

FUN FACT

Your mom or dad might not believe this, but the longest traffic jam ever was over 100 miles long! It was in France in 1980.

I Spy

"I spy with my little eye...a guy named Bob."

EQUIPMENT: None

TO BEGIN: One person is selected to be the first "spy." All the other players go in turn.

TO PLAY: To play this classic car game, the spy says, "I spy with my little eye something starting with..." and then the spy says the first letter of the thing he or she sees. Whatever the spy "spies" must be something that everyone can see. The other players then guess what the spy is looking at. When someone guesses correctly or when everyone gives up, the next player gets to be the spy.

OTHER IDEAS:

- Use something other than letters of the alphabet to describe what you're spying. "I spy...something yellow; something really tall; something with three wheels; something with two names"; and so on.
- Set a time limit for guessing. If no one guesses what the spy is looking at within that time, the spy gets a point.

In Living Color

"Mauve? What color is mauve?"

EQUIPMENT: None

TO BEGIN: One person is selected to be the first King or Queen of Color. All the other players then take turns being the King or Queen of Color.

FUN FACT

The World's Tallest Thermometer? It's 135 feet tall and stands in Baker, California.

TO PLAY: The King or Queen of Color calls out a color. The first player to spot something that is mainly that color gets a point. If no one spots something that is that color in one minute, or one mile, the King or Queen of Color gets the point. Play to as many points as you want. Also, only man-made things count: if green is the color, you can't say you see grass; if it's blue, you can't use the sky as your example. That would make the game too easy.

OTHER IDEAS:

- Along with colors, try using patterns: plaid, stripes, polka-dots, swirls, checks, and so on.
- Make the game harder: To get a point, players have one minute, or one mile, to find three, four, or five things that are the right color.

What-I-Saw Charades

"First word. One syllable. Sounds like...banana?"

EQUIPMENT: None

TO BEGIN: If you have enough people, this game is fun with teams. Four people can make up two teams of two players each. If you have only two or three people, then take turns being the one who does the charades and let all the other players guess.

TO PLAY: Charades is a popular game at parties. You have to use body language and hand gestures—but no words or sounds—to describe something. In this version, you have to act out something you've seen through the window. Once you've picked a secret object, you have one minute to get the other players on your team to guess what it is. Your team gets one point if you're successful; you lose one point if they don't guess it.

OTHER IDEAS:

- Instead of some "thing" you see out the window, choose an action: tractor plowing a field; car making a U-turn; man lowering a flag; horse running in a field; and so on.

HINTS AND EXAMPLES: Here are some of the classic charades clues you can use. Hold up as many fingers as words you're trying to describe. For example, if the mystery object is a station wagon, hold up two fingers. Then, for each word, hold up as many fingers as the word has syllables. The guessers then try to guess each syllable in order, one at a time.

Another clue—pulling on your ear means "sounds like." After you do this, perform an action; players guess what the syllable is that "sounds like" what you did. For example, if you are describing the first syllable of the word *bicycle,* pull on your ear, then point at your eye: the first syllable, *bi*, sounds like "eye." Get it? There really is no right or wrong way to play...just don't make any sounds or use any words while you're doing your charades.

Backseat Baseball

"Two outs, bottom of the ninth.
My brother really needs a big red barn!"

EQUIPMENT: Paper; pencil or pen; the list below.

TO BEGIN: Look at the list on page 30. Things normally seen on car trips are assigned a baseball play. The better you know the list of plays, the faster the game will go.

TO PLAY: For each half-inning, draw a baseball diamond and the four bases on a piece of paper. You're playing a regular, nine-inning baseball game between two teams (you can put more than one player on each team if you have a bunch of people). The baseball play from the list happens as each matching object is spotted by a "team," or a player who is "at bat." For instance, if the team at bat spots a car that is two or more colors, they get a single. But if they spot a mobile home right after that, it's a double play. Move your team around the bases just like in real baseball and see which team scores more runs. Remember, three outs equals one-half inning. Use your drawing of a baseball diamond to mark where runners are and to keep track of how many outs have been made.

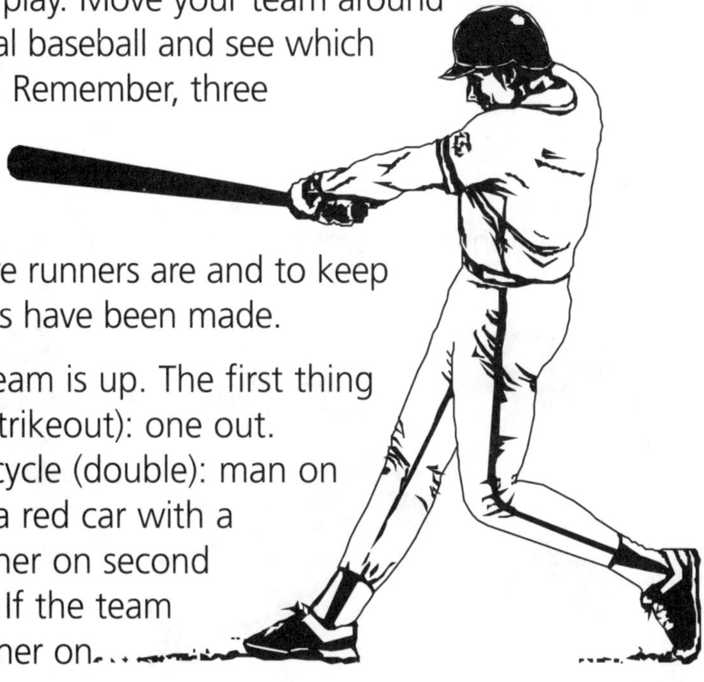

HINTS AND EXAMPLES: Your team is up. The first thing you see is a minivan (strikeout): one out. Then you see a motorcycle (double): man on second. Along comes a red car with a white top (single): runner on second moves to third! (Note: If the team at bat gets a hit, a runner on...

base moves only as many bases as the batter does.) There's a white truck (fly out): two outs. A police car drives by (stolen base): man on second. Then another minivan; drat, three outs. See how it works? Feel free to add additional baseball plays to correspond to additional vehicles, signs, or landmarks!

THE LIST:

OBJECT	BASEBALL PLAY
any car with two or more colors	SINGLE
motorcycle	DOUBLE
motorcycle with two people on it	TRIPLE
red barn	HOME RUN
minivan	STRIKEOUT
mobile home	DOUBLE PLAY*
any all-white car or truck	FLY OUT
any all-blue car or truck	GROUND OUT
any police vehicle	STOLEN BASE

* If no one is on base, then a mobile home is a ground out.

FUN FACT

Want to remember the names of the Great Lakes? Just think of the word HOMES. Huron, Ontario, Michigan, Erie, Superior.

Cool, huh?

Cookin' with Gas

"Dad? How many miles to the gallon does my bike get?"

EQUIPMENT: The list below and sharp eyes

TO BEGIN: Make sure you've got people looking out all the windows. The more area you can cover around the car, the better you'll do.

TO PLAY: Try to spot as many gasoline companies from the list below as you can. Most are nationwide companies, but some are found only in certain parts of the country. If you're taking a long trip across the United States, you might find all of them. Give yourself extra credit for adding names of other gas station companies to the list. Can you find a U Pump? This is a good game to play throughout your trip, not just for one day.

FUN FACT

Before we had cars, people rode horses to get around. Today, Kentucky and Wyoming are the only states with horses on their license plates. In Hawaii, you can still get a license plate for a horse-drawn wagon!

OTHER IDEAS:

- Make up your own lists of businesses to find: fast-food companies, supermarkets, or other nationwide chains, such as Toys R Us, K-mart, and Wal-Mart.

THE LIST: 76, Amoco, BP, Chevron, Citgo, Conoco, Exxon, Marathon, Mobil, Phillips, Shell, Sinclair, Sunoco, Texaco

What the Heck Is That?

"I Know! I Know! It's a flying cow!"

EQUIPMENT: Paper and something to draw with: different colored pencils, pens, or crayons will help.

TO BEGIN: Decide who will be the first "highway artist." The other players will each get a turn.

TO PLAY: The artist looks out the window and sees something he or she can draw. Then the artist tries to draw a picture of the chosen thing; the other players have one minute to guess what it is. Whoever guesses first gets a point, so start guessing the second that pencil hits the paper.

OTHER IDEAS:

- For more silly fun, have everyone draw a head on a piece of paper. Fold the papers so that no one can see what the other players have drawn, but keep the necks visible. Then pass the papers to the right. Now have each person draw a body on the paper that he or she is holding and then fold each paper to hide that part of the drawing. Pass the papers to the right again and have everyone draw legs. Then open the papers to see the funny combination drawings!

Guess What I Saw?

"What color is it? That's not a yes-or-no question!"

EQUIPMENT: None

TO BEGIN: Have you ever heard of Twenty Questions? Well, this is the automobile version. Choose who will go first.

TO PLAY: The chosen player looks outside the car and picks something—the other players have to guess what it is. They can ask up to 20 questions, all of which can be answered only "yes" or "no." If the players guess the object before they run out of questions, they win. If they don't, the first player wins. Everyone takes a turn picking an object for the others to guess; play to any number of points you want.

OTHER IDEAS:

- Make the game harder by allowing only ten questions.
- Allow the person choosing the mystery item to pick not only things but also actions, such as the sun setting, an airplane landing, or a calf getting milk from a cow.

HINTS AND EXAMPLES: For the guessers, try to narrow things down early with questions like, "Is it natural?" or "Is it man-made?" Ask if it is "bigger than a house" or "smaller than a car." Once you start to narrow things down, get more specific: "Have we ever seen it before?" "Do we have one in our hometown?" and so on.

FUN FACT

Bet you've never seen a house made entirely out of dinosaur bones. You can if you go to Medicine Bow, Wyoming.

Faceless Fun

"I just saw a 76 gas station...
but I don't have any 7's or 6's!"

EQUIPMENT: Deck of cards; something to put discards in (a hat or small box)

TO BEGIN: Remove all the face cards (jacks, queens, and kings) from the deck. Then deal out seven cards to each player. (If you have six or more people, decrease the number of cards to five or six—otherwise you'll run out of cards!)

TO PLAY: In each hand, you will have numbered cards and aces. When you see the number on one of your cards somewhere out the windows of the car, put that card in the discard pile. The numbers can be on signs or license plates. When you see a capital A, discard any aces. Small A's don't count—only capital A's. If you have four 3's, you have to see four actual 3's out the window to discard all your 3's. Don't put down all four cards when you see one number 3. If more than one player spots the same A or number, each player may count it. The first player to throw away all his or her cards is the winner.

OTHER IDEAS:

- Sure, the game is called "Faceless Fun," but you can use the face cards if you want. Include them in the cards you deal out. Then, when you see a capital J, Q, or K, toss your Jack, Queen, or King into the discard pile.
- If you have only two or three players, play with more cards each to make the game last longer.
- You can play faces-only, too. Deal the face cards evenly to each player; discard only when you see the words *Jack, Queen,* or *King* out the window. If you pass the right group of fast-food restaurants, the game might be over quickly!

Football Cards

"Penalty. That's illegal use of 'hands.' Get it? Hands? Ha, ha, ha!"

EQUIPMENT: Deck of cards; something to put discards in (a hat or small box); the list below

TO BEGIN: Shuffle the cards. Put them all facedown in a pile. Then choose one player to "receive the football" first.

TO PLAY: This is just like a football game. Each type of card represents a certain play. The first player "with the ball" draws one card. His or her "football team" then does what the card says, according to the list shown here. That team keeps picking until they score (a touchdown or field goal), punt, or make a turnover (a fumble or interception). Then it's the other team's turn. When you have gone through all the cards, shuffle the deck and put them facedown in a pile again. The first team to score 50 or more points wins the game.

THE PLAYS

CARD	FOOTBALL PLAY
ACE	touchdown (7 points)
TWO	punt (lose ball)
THREE	field goal (3 points)
FOUR	incomplete pass (pick again)
FIVE	short running play (pick again)
SIX	fumble (lose ball)
SEVEN	touchdown (7 points)
EIGHT	interception (lose ball)
NINE	short pass (pick again)
TEN	long pass (pick again)
JACK	penalty (pick again)
QUEEN	flea-flicker (pick again)
KING	long running play (pick again)

HINTS AND EXAMPLES: Here is an example of how the game is played.

Player 1 picks a nine. That's a completed short pass. Player 1 picks again and picks a king. That's a long running play. Player 1 picks again and picks a six. That a fumble. Player 1 loses the ball. It's now the other team's turn to pick.

Player 2 picks a four. That's an incomplete pass. Player 2 picks again and picks a five. That's a short running play. Player 2 picks again and picks an ace. That's a touchdown. Player 2 gets seven points. Now the first team gets to pick again.

FUN FACT

Three towns claim to own the World's Largest Ball of String: Darwin, Minnesota; Cawker City, Kansas; and Mountain Springs, Texas. Only Jackson, Wyoming, claims the World's Largest Ball of Barbed Wire.

Twenty

"C'mon three, c'mon three, c'mon three..."

EQUIPMENT: Deck of cards; something to put discards in (a hat or small box)

TO BEGIN: Deal three cards to each player.

FUN FACT

You can see the World's Largest King Kong near Eureka Springs, Arkansas.

TO PLAY: The object is to get exactly 20 points in your hand. Not 21, not 19. Exactly 20. You can have as many cards in your hand as you need, but you win only when they total exactly 20. Each player in turn either discards or picks up a card. Face cards (jacks, queens, and kings) are worth 10; aces can be worth either 1 or 11. You can't both discard and pick up in one turn—just one or the other. Keep picking up or discarding until one player gets exactly 20. Then start again with a new set of three cards. Play as many hands as you like.

OTHER IDEAS:

- No reason you can't play "Thirty" or "Forty"—or any number you choose. Don't make the number too high, though; you'll run out of cards!
- Before you start picking, let each player take one card, without looking at it, from the other players' hands. Or do this every five turns, just to keep things interesting.

HINTS AND EXAMPLES: Remember, you can have more than 20 points in your hand, you just can't be a winner with that hand. For example, say you have 17 points in your hand and one of your cards is a 4. On your next turn, you draw a 7. That makes 24. But on the turn after that, you can discard the 4 to make 20 and you're a winner!

Mystery "Face" Cards

"Um, is the mystery card red?"

EQUIPMENT: Deck of cards; as many foreheads as players

TO BEGIN: Each player is dealt five cards facedown. No peeking!

TO PLAY: Each player takes a turn holding up one card on his or her forehead, face out. When it's your turn, you get to ask yes-or-no questions as you try to guess the card on your forehead—you can ask four questions for each card. For every card you guess after you ask your four questions, you get one point. Whoever gets the most correct guesses out of his or her five cards is the winner.

FUN FACT

When you drive through Providence, Rhode Island, watch out for the World's Largest Bug. She's a 58-foot-long termite (okay, she's a statue), and her name is Nibbles Woodaway. Get it?

HINTS AND EXAMPLES: Here are some good questions to ask the other players:

- Is the card red? (If the answer is no, the card must be black.)
- Is it a face card? (If the answer is no, it must be a number card or an ace.)
- If the card is a number, is it higher than or equal to 6? (If the answer is no, the number is either 2, 3, 4, or 5.)

You have to be a combination of detective and fortune teller to guess the cards. Practice this game a few times and you'll get pretty good at it.

Go Fish

"Do you have any twelves? Just Kidding!"

EQUIPMENT: Deck of cards

TO BEGIN: The car version of Go Fish is played with two players. Deal seven cards to each player. Place the rest of the cards in a pile facedown between you.

TO PLAY: The object of the game is to gather pairs of the same cards. Twos go with twos, fives with fives, kings with kings, and so on. The player who goes first puts down any pairs he or she has. Then that player asks the other player, "Do you have any ____?" Fill in the blank with a card that will match one you have in your hand. If the other player has any, he or she has to give them to you. If the other player doesn't have any, he or she says, "Go fish!" Then you draw one card from the facedown pile that sits on the seat between you. Every time you get a pair, put it down. If you can't make a pair from the other player's card or from fishing in the facedown pile, it is the other player's turn. The first player to run out of cards wins. Remember, you have to have at least one of a card before you can ask for it.

OTHER IDEAS:

- Play four-of-a-kind instead of pairs.
- Play "Blind Fish." Every other turn, instead of asking the other player for a card, just pick one from his or her hand at random. You might catch the fish you're looking for, or you might get something you just want to throw back!

Full Car...Empty Hands

"I just saw a parking lot with every car—
I mean, card—in my hand... I'm an instant winner!"

EQUIPMENT: Deck of cards; something to put discards in (a hat or small box); the list below

TO BEGIN: Deal each player seven cards.

TO PLAY: Each card value in the deck is assigned a type of vehicle or sight out the window. As each thing that matches up with one of your cards is seen, discard that card. The first player with "empty hands," or no cards, is the winner. Feel free to change the list to vary the game.

OTHER IDEAS:

- Play with more players and fewer cards for really fast-paced games.
- Play with more cards per player if you're a twosome.
- Add a "wild card." If anyone spots, say, a purple Volkswagon van, he or she gets to throw away any two cards. Or have a "negative wild card." If your car passes any billboard with the word *food* on it, everyone has to pick another card from the discard pile.

THE LIST:

CARD	MATCH
ACE	yellow car
TWO	pickup truck
THREE	minivan
FOUR	car the same make as yours
FIVE	18-wheeler
SIX	McDonald's
SEVEN	gas station
EIGHT	blue car
NINE	red car
TEN	motorcycle
JACK	any license plate with a J on it
QUEEN	any car or truck with two or more people in it
KING	bus

How Long Is a Mile?

"My sister sure thinks this mile is long. No, wait...she fell asleep!"

EQUIPMENT: Odometer; someone in the front seat to watch it (preferably not the driver!)

TO BEGIN: The odometer (oh-DOM-it-er) is the line of numbers on your car's dashboard that tells how many miles you've driven. To practice, watch the odometer go from one mile to the next. Use the last two numbers on the right; these usually measure miles and tenths of a mile.

TO PLAY: This is an easy and sort of silly game. When the number measuring tenths of a mile reads zero, the person watching the odometer says, "Go!" Close your eyes. Open them when you think you've traveled exactly a mile—the number measuring tenths of a mile should be back at zero. See who can come the closest to guessing how long it takes to drive a mile.

OTHER IDEAS:

- If all the players agree beforehand, try to distract the guesser. Hum a tune, count really fast, or try to make the guesser laugh.
- If you get really good at guessing a mile, try guessing two or three miles.

FUN FACT

You can stand in four states at once in only one place in America–at Four Corners, where Arizona, Colorado, Utah, and New Mexico meet.

Rock, Paper, Scissors

"Does rock cut paper or do scissors break up rock?"

EQUIPMENT: Your hands

TO BEGIN: This is a good game to use to make decisions. Instead of flipping a coin to see who gets the front seat or who gets the last cookie, use this game.

TO PLAY: All players should hold one hand behind their backs. Then together count, "1-2-3-shoot!" When you say "shoot," put your hand out in front of you in one of three ways:

ROCK: Make a fist

PAPER: Hold your hand out flat with fingers together

SCISSORS: Make a V with your first two fingers

If all the players do the same thing with their hands, try it again. If not, here's how you determine the winner:

PAPER COVERS ROCK: Paper wins

ROCK BREAKS SCISSORS: Rock wins

SCISSORS CUT PAPER: Scissors wins

That's pretty much it. You can also play best two-out-of-three.

HINTS AND EXAMPLES: Each of the three choices has an equal chance to win—but don't give your opponent an edge by using a pattern. Don't always go paper, rock, scissors over and over, for example. Mix it up. Do the same thing a few times in a row, then suddenly switch. You can't really get better at this game...just luckier!

One-Double-Oh

"I just saw a UFO! I win automatically."

EQUIPMENT: Paper; pencil or pen; the list below

TO BEGIN: Study the list of items below. The better you know what to look for, the better you'll do. You can also add items to the list, if you want. Be creative.

TO PLAY: Using the points and vehicles listed below, try to be the first to spot at least 100 points' worth of objects out the car windows. Make sure to call out when you see something on the list; if two people call out at the same time, neither gets points. Play as many rounds as you like. You can even hold a tournament throughout the trip, with new games every day.

THE LIST

OBJECT	POINTS
FOUR-DOOR CAR	1
PICKUP TRUCK	3
RV (BIG CAMPER)	3
SPORT-UTILITY VEHICLE (SUV)	5
DOG IN PICKUP TRUCK	6
STATION WAGON	6
MOTORCYCLE	8
BICYCLE	10
POLICE CAR OR HIGHWAY PATROL CAR	13
FIRE ENGINE (STOPPED OR MOVING)	15
AMBULANCE	15
HELICOPTER	20
MOTORCYCLE WITH SIDECAR	25
HOT-AIR BALLOON	25
HORSE-DRAWN WAGON	25
POLICE CAR OR HIGHWAY PATROL CAR BEHIND YOU	50
UFO	1 million*

(*Instant all-time champion)

OTHER IDEAS:

- Play "One-Double-Oh-on-the-Dot." In this version, you have to get exactly 100 points.

Sixty-Second Story

"Okay, I'll go first.
'Debbie woke up to find she had become a cockroach.'"

EQUIPMENT: A digital watch or a watch with a second hand; your imagination. A small, portable tape recorder would be fun to have, too, but it's not necessary.

TO BEGIN: Turn off the radio while you play this game…it'll be easier.

TO PLAY: The object is to create a complete story in one minute (60 seconds). Each person in the car adds one sentence at a time. It doesn't have to be a serious story or a real story or even make much sense. It just has to begin and end in one minute. At the end of a minute, start a new story. If you have a tape recorder handy, the stories you've created are often even funnier when you play them back.

HINTS AND EXAMPLES: The first sentence is important. It should set the mood and character or characters of the story. It should allow for something to happen. "The dog bit me" isn't as good a first sentence as "The giant blue dog growled at me as I went into the room.…" This game is kind of strange the first time you play it, but once you get going, you'll turn into fans. It's really fun.

FUN FACT

The only license plate in North America that is not rectangular is from Canada's Northwest Territories. The plates there are shaped like a polar bear!

And Then I Packed the...

"Ooh, I can't remember what came after the penguin and the cantaloupe!"

EQUIPMENT: A silly sense of humor

TO PLAY: This is a memory game. The first person to go says, "I packed the _________ in the suitcase." The blank is any noun. And we do mean any. What you're packing doesn't really have to fit into a suitcase. The next person says, "I packed the _______ and the _______ in the suitcase." That person has to say exactly what the first person "packed" then add his or her own new thing. After three or four people have gone, it starts to be a challenge to remember all the things that are going in that suitcase. The first person who can't name all the things in the suitcase in the proper order is out. Then start a new game with the remaining players until only one is left.

HINTS AND EXAMPLES: Here is an example of the first few rounds of a game.

PLAYER 1: I packed a rabbit in the suitcase.

PLAYER 2: I packed a rabbit and my socks in the suitcase.

PLAYER 3: I packed a rabbit and my socks and Uncle Joe's umbrella in the suitcase.

PLAYER 4: I packed a rabbit and my socks and Uncle Joe's umbrella and the state of Michigan in the suitcase.

PLAYER 1: I packed a rabbit and my socks and Uncle Joe's umbrella and the state of Michigan and a penguin in the suitcase.

As Far as You Can See

"I think that giant radio tower is eight million miles away. Do I win?"

EQUIPMENT: An odometer

TO BEGIN: Looking out the front of the car, choose an object way in the distance that everyone can see. It can be a giant sign, a water tower, a radio tower, a church steeple, a bridge, or whatever.

TO PLAY: Each player guesses how far away the chosen landmark is. Whoever comes closest to guessing without going over the distance is the winner. Use the car's odometer to measure the distance.

OTHER IDEAS:

- To make it more challenging, the players should guess in tenths of a mile, as in, "That giant plastic cow is one and six-tenths miles away."
- Play this game while you're playing others. If you pick something that's quite far away, you can play other games while you track the distance to the object in this game.

Speed Demons

"Um, it's really dark...are we going faster than the speed of light?"

EQUIPMENT: A speedometer; a watch with a second hand or a digital watch will come in handy, too.

TO BEGIN: Simple. Close your eyes.

TO PLAY: With their eyes closed, players guess the car's exact speed. Give each player ten seconds to decide the speed. Play ten rounds and see who can come closest the most often.

FUN FACT

The Romans laid out more than 5,000 miles of roads from Scotland to what is now Israel. Each road was wide enough for six Roman soldiers to walk side by side.

OTHER IDEAS:

- To make it interesting, have your driver slow down slightly or speed up a bit (while staying under the speed limit, of course) for each round.

Thumb Wrestling

"Dad! That guy from the WWF keeps winning all the thumb-wrestling matches! Make him stop!"

EQUIPMENT: Thumbs—one per player

TO BEGIN: Make a hook with your first four fingers, leaving your thumb sticking straight up. Then hook those fingers with your opponent's. Both players need to use the same hand, right or left.

TO PLAY: With your hands hooked together, perform the official thumb-wrestling countdown. Touch your thumb on the other person's finger, then yours, then his, counting together out loud, "One, two, three." When you get to three, begin wrestling. The object is to pin your opponent's thumb under yours for a quick three-count without unhooking your hands. Play over and over until your parents threaten to leave you at the next rest stop.

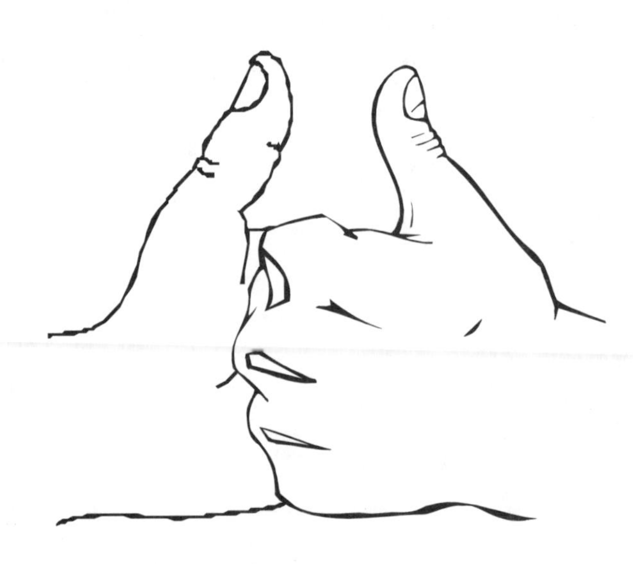

Heart of Dixie
PLI021
Alabama

ALASKA

ARIZONA
TCMPL

Arkansas
ROOLTF
The Natural State

California
3M1X21

XBI-213
COLORADO

CONNECTICUT
THI-ELT
PRESERVE THE SOUND

THE FIRST STATE
241571
DELAWARE

FLORIDA
SVI OIP
DMV
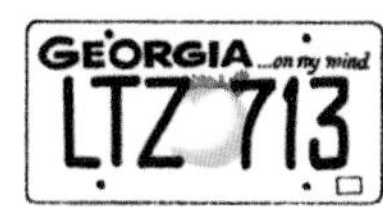
GEORGIA ...on my mind
LTZ 713

HAWAII
NTE 281
ALOHA STATE

IDAHO
BLBRD
Wildlife

Illinois
Land of Lincoln
LTH-493

INDIANA
12A4894

Iowa
MAI 041
LINN

SN KANSAS
95
PMI 440

Kentucky
SAO 518
FRANKLIN

Louisiana
BTP 673
SPORTSMAN'S PARADISE

MAINE
PRZ TIZ
Vacationland

Maryland
TEH PZE
Treasure the Chesapeake

Massachusetts
IAT RLF
The Spirit of America

MICHIGAN
DTI-VPL
GREAT LAKES

EXPLORE Minnesota
246 AXP
10,000 lakes

MISSISSIPPI
TLI 219

MISSOURI
ZRI 414
SHOW-ME STATE

142 UTJ
100 YEARS
MONTANA

NEBRASKA
NPSTEH

NEVADA
PLTVAN
125 YEARS OF VISION
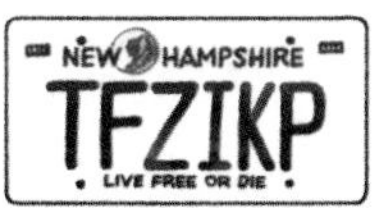
NEW HAMPSHIRE
TFZIKP
LIVE FREE OR DIE

New Jersey
EFR 168
Garden State

217 AAR
New Mexico USA
Land of Enchantment

NEW YORK
NMI 071
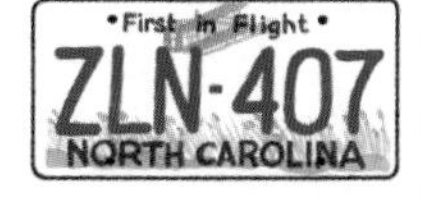
First in Flight
ZLN-407
NORTH CAROLINA

Discover the Spirit
DTIMWN
NORTH DAKOTA

OHIO
AWI 524

OKLAHOMA
MSI DTA
NATIVE AMERICA

Oregon
ATJ 674

PENNSYLVANIA
SLN PTI
KEYSTONE STATE

Rhode Island
RFN 627
Ocean State

Nothing Could Be Finer
DXC 258
South Carolina

South Dakota
AVN 575
GREAT FACES, GREAT PLACES

BicenTENNial
95
XCT ONJ

TEXAS
342 THT
THE LONE STAR STATE

UTAH
524 YZA
1896 CENTENNIAL 1996

GREEN MOUNTAINS
456179
VERMONT

VIRGINIA
AMJ 115

Washington
681-ABI

West Virginia
1A 4747
Wild, Wonderful
96

WISCONSIN
JLTZRY
America's Dairyland

Wyoming
9 1642

Alberta
AKB 174
Wild Rose Country
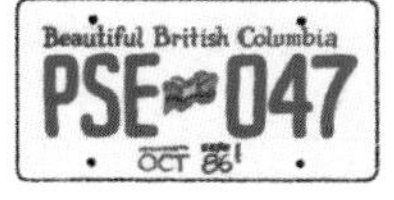
Beautiful British Columbia
PSE 047
OCT 86

Friendly Manitoba
JRV 542
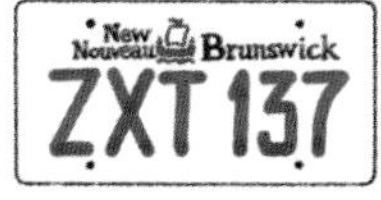
New Nouveau Brunswick
ZXT 137

Newfoundland & Labrador
PLT 923

NOVA SCOTIA
EIM 028
CANADA'S OCEAN PLAYGROUND

ONTARIO
SLT214
YOURS TO DISCOVER

Birthplace of Confederation
13 PNY
Prince Edward Island

Québec
791 AWT
Je me souviens

Saskatchewan
NIM 261

ONE WAY

The Klondike
4430
Yukon

EXPLORE CANADA'S ARCTIC
823
NORTHWEST TERRITORIES

ONE WAY